CAMEOS
OF CHURCH
HISTORY

Richard A. Boever, C.SS.R.

LIGUORI
PUBLICATIONS

One Liguori Drive
Liguori, Missouri 63057
(314) 464-2500

Imprimi Potest:
John F. Dowd, C.SS.R.
Provincial, St. Louis Province
Redemptorist Fathers

Imprimatur:
+ Edward J. O'Donnell
Vicar General, Archdiocese of St. Louis

ISBN 0-89243-249-7

Table of Contents

PART III: THE REFORMATION

PART IV: THE MODERN ERA

Introduction

For many students, the study of history ranks high on the list of "most-boring subjects"; exams in history are counted among the worst. Who can remember all the trivial names and dates and what they have to do with modern life?

The study of history, however, need not be such a bad experience. If the focus of study is on understanding human responses and reactions to specific events and circumstances, the lessons of history can have a broadening effect. In Church history, when we zero in on the experiences of fellow believers from the past and move beyond the details to the reasons why people acted the way they did, we are better able to understand ourselves and our times.

For history to have an impact on us, then, it is essential to understand human nature. This is what the author of the Book of Genesis did when he wrote about the beginning of all history — the creation of the world — and his account is still the bedrock philosophy of our beliefs.

At the very foundation of all history is the fact that it is the work of God. Things are not the way they are by accident. God set the whole process in motion in the great work of creation, and his providence guides it still. Because this world is the work of God it is good.

In the hierarchy of creation, men and women have a special place; they are created in the very image of God. The human person is the supreme work of creation and, as such, is given authority over the earth: "Be fertile and multiply; fill the earth and subdue it. Have dominion over the fish of the sea, the birds of the air, and all the living things that move on the earth" (Genesis 1:28). In the Christian perception of our place in the universe, we are very significant.

Although God created the world with a particular plan, his creatures failed to follow his original design. This detour was possible because God gave people free will. They were (and we are) free to cooperate with God's plan or to go against it. In the Book of Genesis, the account of the fall of Adam and Eve and their expulsion from Paradise makes the point that people used (and use) their freedom to rebel against God. This we call sin, and sin is a reality in our world.

In spite of the fact that human beings refused (and refuse) to follow the plan God intended for their own growth and that of the perfection of the world, God did not (and does not) give up on his creation. Immediately after the fall of Adam and Eve, God promised a Savior who would redeem the world. (See Genesis 3:15.) This Redeemer is Jesus Christ, who not only restored the vision given substance by the Creator but also bestowed the power to make that vision a reality.

These "basics" of human life are at work through all generations of human history. They can be identified in world movements and in each individual life. If we can keep these elements in perspective and see how they intermingled in the past, we will understand history — the record of the struggle between good and evil within human nature and in human times. People of the past, like ourselves, were blessed by the providence of God that led them — and cursed by the remnants of sin that plagued them. They had to respond to specific moments and events in time, trying "by the sweat of their brows" to come to conclusions and decisions that were pleasing to the plan of God. In this process, in the interplay of divine protection and human sinfulness, doctrines were defined, wars were fought, and works of charity were inaugurated. When we are able to understand how historical events happened in past centuries, we stand a better chance of developing some insight into why things are happening as they are today.

PART I
THE BEGINNINGS

1 Birth of the Church

Pictures of a mother lovingly holding her infant in her arms quite often appear in the daily newspaper. They usually show the mother looking into the baby's eyes as if to say, ''What will become of you?''

When a child is born into the world, he or she is gifted with a certain amount of talent, intelligence, and dexterity to accomplish the tasks of life. The child is also limited by human nature and by an environment that may or may not promote the full flowering of the total potential. It is the combination of the individual's gifts and limitations, along with God's grace, that produces the final results.

Jesus, in a manner of speaking, gave birth to his Church; and in his very human concern, he must have felt parental anxiety for his little flock. Read, for example, chapters 14 to 17 from John's Gospel, which record Jesus' discourse the night before he died. He wanted to tell his infant Church so much. He wanted the best for his people, but he also knew the temptations his followers would have to weather. He consoled his disciples with the promise that, though he would not be with them much longer, he would not leave them orphans. He would send them his Holy Spirit, and he promised to remain with them always.

After almost two thousand years, Jesus' message still goes out to all the world, and his presence is still felt within the Church. There have been difficult moments, but the Holy Spirit has led his people through the centuries and continues to instruct them in everything.

The first Christians did not inherit an organization with ready-made bylaws. Only in time, by responding to the circumstances of daily life and by discerning with their own minds and hearts the direction of the

Holy Spirit, would they come to understand the direction in which God was leading them.

The Gospel shows us that from the very first days of the Church the Body of Christ was made up of both human and divine elements. The disciples went to the upstairs room of the place where they were staying and devoted themselves to constant prayer. They must have wondered if they had been mistaken in their allegiance to Jesus. Perhaps they would meet the same fate. In time, many of them would drink from the same cup, but only after being strengthened by the grace of God.

It was in this atmosphere of doubt and fear that the mighty power of God made itself manifest:

> Suddenly from up in the sky there came a noise like a strong, driving wind which was heard all through the house where they were seated. Tongues as of fire appeared, which parted and came to rest on each of them. All were filled with the Holy Spirit. They began to express themselves in foreign tongues and make bold proclamation as the Spirit prompted them (Acts 2:2-4).

The descent of the Holy Spirit on Pentecost is celebrated as the "Birthday of the Church." On that day, the minds of the disciples were opened. They saw Jesus in a new light and understood so many of the things he had said to them. Their attitudes were changed from that of withdrawal to a new boldness in proclaiming the Word of God. Things would not always be easy; but with God's help, no problem would be insurmountable. The Church would meet the challenge of the centuries. The Holy Spirit would direct his people through the course of human history into the Kingdom of God.

The history of God's Church had begun.

2 Three Patterns of Early Christianity

The universe is growing smaller. It is possible to talk or even to travel to the other side of the world in "no time at all." But things weren't always that way. The small town was the basic community — the family's food was bought from the local market, and justice was executed in the town square. When a visitor passed through the village, people would gather to hear stories of faraway places. It is not surprising, then, that as Christianity first spread through the civilized world of the first centuries distinct "brands" of the religion could be found. The local culture had a great influence on the worship and belief of the people. And this was very evident as Christianity spread from Palestine to the Greek and Roman world.

The people of Palestine were the original Christians; they were the first to hear the Good News. In the years immediately following the death of Christ, Jewish Christianity had its own distinct flavor and its own approach to God. Jewish Christians suffered difficulties from fellow Jews when they refused to join a rebellion against Rome. In the first century, they were even forced to abandon Jerusalem as their center. Edessa (in southwestern Asia) became prominent, and a strong community developed there.

For this Christian community, religion was primarily a "way of love." God had compassion and tenderness, qualities our culture usually attributes to the feminine side of personality. In fact, the Hebrew term for "Word" — as in Jesus, the Word of God — was feminine in gender. Religion was primarily a life lived in love, and Jesus was the divine Model of this way of life.

In the Greek world, Christianity took on its own distinct characteristics. Saint Paul, the great missionary who broke cultural barriers by bringing a Jewish religion to the pagan world, did much to bring a "foreign religion" into a Greek mentality. In part because of Paul's strong personality but even more because of the refined Greek culture, Christianity emerged in the Greek world as a unique expression of the same religion lived in Edessa. Alexandria, in Egypt, eventually became the central city for this form of Christianity.

For the Greek mind, so interested in philosophy, Christianity had to be understood in terms of metaphysics. The Greeks were captivated by the notion of "being." Jesus was the Wisdom of God, Being itself made flesh, and the Communicator of divine wisdom. The greatest problem for these philosophical theologians was in coming to grips with how Jesus could be an ordinary human being. This community placed great importance on the mind. Faith meant believing correctly and living accordingly. Therefore, great emphasis was put on creeds and dogma.

As the Christian religion continued to move westward, the converts of Rome accepted and practiced the faith with their own style. Rome, with the great tradition of justice and law, gave Christianity an inheritance of morals. Christ was the greatest of all lawgivers. He was often depicted as holding the hand raised, with two fingers extended, in a gesture familiar to Roman courts of law. Tertullian and Augustine, both lawyers, were the great spokesmen of these Christians.

Roman Christianity was interested in the problems of human nature. As a result, ethics and morals became central. For these Christians, Jesus was the perfect man; and heresies that developed in the West always centered around difficulties in understanding how Jesus could be God and, at the same time, be totally human.

These three forms of Christianity existed side by side in the Catholic Church. All three approaches have had an impact on our religious practice today. Christianity transcends any single culture. Salvation is not limited to one way of understanding reality. The Church is for all people in all times.

3 Early Definition of Doctrines

The era of the Fathers of the Church, the first six centuries of Christian history, ranks among the greatest in our heritage. It was an important time when, under the inspiration of the Holy Spirit, great minds debated weighty matters. These were the years when many of the basic doctrines of our Church were defined and put into the Creeds we recite today.

Jesus came, in the fullness of time, to give us salvation and to reveal to us the glory of God. His teachings were recorded in the New Testament, and by faith Christians were able to accept a way of life. Questions surfaced, however, that required further explanation. It was the Creeds that further defined the teachings of faith. The Age of the Fathers was the time when the great Creeds were written.

In the first centuries after Christ, people wondered how "God worked." There could only be one God, yet Jesus spoke of his Father and the Holy Spirit. The living belief of the Christian community affirmed a plurality in God — Father, Son, and Holy Spirit. This can be seen both in liturgical documents, particularly baptismal rituals, and in statements of belief. How did this plurality in God jibe with the basic belief in the oneness of God?

Many great theological debates, and not a few heresies, sprang from questions concerning the nature of God, but it was not until the year 325, at the Council of Nicaea, that the definition of the Trinity was clearly stated. In the one God there are three Persons — the Father, the Son, and the Holy Spirit.

During these early centuries, Christian thinkers engaged in varied discussions about the true nature of Jesus. Some said Jesus was totally divine; he only looked like a man. Others said that Jesus was just a man, but the nature of God floated over him and gave him special powers. Still others said the Spirit of God infused the man Jesus, but only at certain times; God, for instance, did not die on the Cross, only the man Jesus died. Some wondered if Jesus was not a "secondary god," less than the Father but more than a human being — a kind of go-between with the Father for humankind.

It's hard for a twentieth-century Christian to realize that for centuries the nature of the Savior was debated. Like the nature of the Trinity, which we so routinely recite in the Profession of Faith every Sunday, we take for granted the human and divine natures of Christ. But at the Council of Chalcedon, in the year 451, the nature of Christ was still being defined. He was truly God and truly man: one person with two natures, divine and human.

Since the nature of Jesus was a subject of debate, we ought to expect that confusion would also arise over the place of his mother, Mary. Some attributed to Mary the motherhood of only a part of Jesus. They argued that she was mother only of his human body, not his divinity. Saint Cyril responded that Christ is not a man in whom the Word descended but the Word himself, born in a flesh that is his own. Jesus' humanity did not exist separately. Since Christ is not two separate persons, one human and one divine, Mary is not the mother of only a part of Jesus. Therefore, Mary is rightfully called and is the Mother of God.

As these three examples of doctrine show, the Fathers of the Church had to tackle some of the greatest questions of our faith. For that reason, these first centuries are, indeed, honored years in Church history. The Creeds we use today came from this age. It was a time of faith seeking understanding, and that understanding has been bequeathed to us as our tradition of faith.

4 World Reaction to Christianity

The first people to hear the Good News of Jesus Christ were the Jews. Even when Paul, the Apostle of the Gentiles, moved beyond Palestine, he first proclaimed the gospel in the synagogue, the place of worship for the Jews. Many became Christians.

As Christianity continued to grow, non-Jews also believed the gospel. Debate arose over whether or not it was necessary for Gentile believers to become Jews before being baptized as Christians. This was the first matter of discipline requiring a decision from the Church at large.

The leaders of the Church met in Jerusalem to consider the issue. (An account of the discernment of the apostles in this matter can be found in Acts of the Apostles, chapter 15.) This was not an easy matter to decide. Strong opinions were held on both sides of the issue, but the outcome was that it was not necessary for converts to be Jews before being baptized. As with every change, there is both gain and loss in the decision. In this case, the rich heritage of Judaism would be less influential on the new faith; but the Church became an independent religion, claiming for itself the title "New Israel" along with the heritage of the Old Testament.

When Christianity became separate from the Jewish structure, the Church also lost the privileges of Roman law accorded to "legal religions." Christians were, in fact, viewed with suspicion. They were accused of horrible crimes, including cannibalism and incest. They became the scapegoats for many of the troubles of the Roman Empire.

Eventually, Christians were subjected to persecution. The severity of these punishments varied from place to place and from time to time.

In the year 64, Nero ordered the first persecution of Christians by the State. He blamed them for a great fire that destroyed parts of Rome. From that time onward, a persecution against the Christians happened approximately every fifty years. At times, these persecutions were the result of the vanity of the emperor, who wanted to be venerated as a god. The persecutions also served the Romans as a means of increasing their treasuries when funds were dwindling. A persecution allowed the government to confiscate the property of wealthier Christians for itself. Finally, ignorance also has to be included as a reason for persecution. Human beings try to stamp out what they cannot understand. Since religion plays a part in the stability of any society, when the Romans witnessed the growing numbers in Christian ranks, fears were voiced that the religion of the State, and therefore the stability of society itself, was in jeopardy.

It was not until the year 311, under the Emperor Constantine, that Christianity became a tolerated religion. Freedom of worship for Christians became the official policy of the State. Christians rose to high positions in the government, and the emperor himself was baptized. Christianity became the established religion of the empire.

The new status of the Church brought with it a new phase in history. No longer were Christians required to be as serious about their conversion, since Baptism no longer carried with it the possibility of persecutions as it had in the past. As a result, there were some who took Baptism lightly. On the other hand, many of the barriers that had hindered the spread of the gospel were now lifted, and a new peace existed for the Christian people. In this peace, the weighty matters of theology could be constructively debated, and the doctrine of the Church was formulated for Christians. This doctrine endures to this day.

5 Roots of Religious Life

At the present time (in the 1980s) there are approximately 150,000 Sisters, Brothers, and priests in the United States who have taken religious vows. Most Catholics are familiar with members of religious orders. They might know a contemplative, who prays for the Church day and night; or a scholar, who teaches one of the sacred and secular sciences; or a missionary, who works to preach the gospel in a foreign land; or a medical professional, who helps bring the healing of Christ to the ill; or a pastoral minister, who nourishes the spiritual life of the parish community. The variety of this selective list proves that it is not the work itself that gives the sense of identity to the religious life. Something more basic is at the root of this lifestyle in the Church.

Religious life did not always exist, and this fact gives a direction in discovering what is at the foundation of the life. If the reason for the evolution of the lifestyle can be identified, we will better understand who the religious are in the Church.

In the first three centuries of existence, the Church grew in the midst of opposition and persecution. The ultimate surrender of faith was to follow the gospel even to the point of martyrdom, the highest grace for the Christian. In martyrdom, the Christian perfectly imitated the Redeemer by giving his or her life for the sake of the gospel. When the persecutions ended in the early fourth century, death no longer threatened the Christian. Christianity became socially and culturally acceptable, and some Christians lived the gospel in less than an inspiring manner. Yet, there were those who sought a distinct kind of dedication to the Savior, akin to what martyrdom had been in past centuries. Men and women of high ideals chose to go to the desert. Monasticism began.

The desert represented the ideal location for those who sought a life of intense dedication. Men and women went there to embrace the solitary life. In this way, they escaped what was becoming, in their judgment, a pagan culture. But the desert was appealing not just because it was a barren wasteland, free from corrupt society. In the empty places, belief had it, demons lived; and the early solitaries wanted to make warfare with these enemies of their Lord. In warfare with the devils, they could become the men and women God had created them to be. They could strive for ideal humanity, as God intended it to be before the Fall from grace. The victory of Christ over death made such a life possible.

Many men and women ventured into the deserts of Egypt and other abandoned areas. Saint Anthony gathered many to himself and taught them the solitary way of life. In time, some of these individuals gathered together, and a community life emerged. Saint Pachomius led this cenobitical reform, as it was called, giving people who lived alone an opportunity to receive the sacraments and pray together. With Pachomius, community life became one of the elements of this lifestyle. In the West, Saint Benedict would build on these traditions in his Rule; and other founders of religious orders would adapt the experiences of these early monks and nuns to the situations of their times.

Today, religious still seek a life of dedication within a community where a simple lifestyle is the norm and goods are held in common. This they do by their vow, or promise, of poverty. They live a life of celibacy in order to serve the whole family of God. This they do by a dedication to chastity. And, by obedience, they strive to discern the needs of the Church and their own needs in consultation with religious superiors and in a spirit of self-sacrifice. The men and women of religious life, in the long tradition of dedicated service, respond to the call of Christ to follow him in a special way.

6 Our Eastern Heritage

Most Roman Catholics give little thought to the Byzantine contribution to our Western Church. A limited perspective is a difficulty in human nature. We know best that with which we are familiar, but a bit of information on the wealth of our inheritance from the Byzantine Empire might serve as a springboard for a broader vision.

In the days of Roman emperors, Constantine the Great moved the capital of the empire from Rome to Constantinople, formerly known as the city of Byzantium. As the "New Rome," this Patriarchal See found a new prestige and exerted a tremendous influence on Christianity for the next eleven centuries. The date of the founding of Constantinople, now called Istanbul, was A.D. 324. While Italy was besieged by the barbarians and Western society entered a time known as the Dark Ages, this great capital of Asia Minor would have a history and cultural development of its own. Even after the city lost its influence, many of the rich traditions continued, especially in the heritage of Eastern Rite Catholics and Orthodox Christians.

The Eastern Empire had three major periods. The first was the time of greatest importance and richest development: "It integrated Christianity within the Greco-Roman tradition; it defined Christian dogma and set up the structures of Christian life; it created a Christian literature and a Christian art" (Cyril Mango, *Byzantium*).

The second period of the Byzantine Empire was the time of the rise of Islam. In the seventh century, the Christian empire suffered a catastrophic attack from the invading Arab Moslems. The Christian empire lost great territories and political power. So great was the loss that it never recovered its former strength, and a backward-look attitude, dreaming of what had been, became more dominant. The greatest positive outcome of this period was that, with the loss of the great territories surrounding the Mediterranean Sea, the Byzantine Empire looked to less settled areas of the North and West for expansion. Great missionary activity brought Christianity as far as Moravia and the Baltic Sea.

The last period of the Byzantine Empire was the time between the eleventh and the fifteenth century, a time of decline and loss, including the pillage of Constantinople by the Fourth Crusade. By 1453, when the city fell to the Turks, the great centers of government and culture had moved elsewhere.

In the year 1054, the great crack in Christian unity, which persists to this day, took place. The Catholic and the Orthodox Church divided. Political, theological, and cultural differences precipitated the split. Following the Dark Ages, as modern Europe began to emerge with a newfound strength, Western Christianity had less to do with the East, which by then was in a time of decline. The sacking of the capital by Catholic Crusaders added to the rift between the two centers of Christianity. Theological controversy grew over the issues of papal power, the date of Easter, and the addition of a phrase into the Nicene Creed by the West. Eventually, the tension became so great that the Roman pope and the Orthodox patriarch mutually excommunicated each other and their respective followers. (Eastern Rite Catholics, also called Uniates because of their union with Rome, are different from members of the Eastern Orthodox Church whose leaders separated from the Catholic Church in A.D. 1054.)

Great strides have been made toward the reunion of the Catholic and the Orthodox Churches. Modern popes have met with patriarchs; and Vatican II emphasized the honored place of Eastern Rite Catholics. The history of Byzantium deserves a special place in Catholic history, and even the forces of history can be reversed by the power of the Holy Spirit.

7 Controversy Over Veneration of Images

Most Catholics have heard, at one time or another, the accusation that having statues in the church is wrong. The pointing finger of condemnation goes so far as to claim that we Catholics worship these images. Such statements make for wrinkled foreheads, filled with question marks, for most of us. These critics are certainly off the mark, at least for the vast majority of the faithful. But the arguments are not new. The same issues were debated in the eighth and ninth centuries.

At that time, great controversy arose over the representation of the human figure for devotional purposes. In the early 700s, two bishops of Asia Minor questioned the respect given to images (icons). The Roman emperor, Leo III, backed the two bishops and by the year 726 indicated that he wanted all images to be destroyed. To enforce his opinion he brought so much pressure upon the patriarch of Constantinople, Germanus, that in the year 730 the bishop was forced to resign his See; and the destruction of crucifixes, icons, and reliquaries began.

The destruction of sacred images was not universal. Some areas responded to the order more wholeheartedly than others. A number of influential people opposed the order. Saint John Damascene wrote articles for the bishop of Jerusalem, defending the images; the popes of Rome, politically still under the emperor, vehemently disagreed with him in letters; and the monks and civil servants of Constantinople also resisted the emperor in this matter.

It is difficult to say precisely why the opposition to the images surfaced. The influence of Islam had some bearing. Since the seventh century, the new religion had become very powerful in the Eastern

Empire, and the Moslems strictly forbade any images. In Asia Minor, where iconoclasm (the movement to destroy all images) was strongest, there were a number of groups that had a history of being unfavorable toward icons. The emperor's family itself came from a region where the Monophysite heresy was strong, and he probably never experienced the respect and reverence other people felt toward their icons. (The Monophysite heresy taught that Jesus had only a divine nature, not a human nature.) Naturally, the group was not interested in pictures that represented the human nature of the Son of God. All these circumstances had some weight in the emperor's opposition to the images.

The theological reasons for opposing the veneration of icons never carried much weight. It was only after the destruction was common that the theologians sought reasons to justify the actions. The iconoclasts argued that an image of Christ was itself heretical because no picture could capture both the divine and human nature of Jesus. One or the other nature would have to be downplayed. Neither could the saints be pictured in art, for now they were in a glorious state, no longer bound by physical matter.

For almost a century the controversy raged over whether or not to permit images. The Council of Nicaea II restored a reverenced place to icons in 787, but the decision was reversed at the Synod of Hagia Sophia in 815. It was not until 843 that the tide turned permanently and it was once again permitted to represent holy things, events, and people in art forms. This event is still celebrated every year by churches under the Patriarch of Constantinople as the feast of Orthodoxy.

Sincere men and women found themselves on both sides of the iconoclasm controversy. Although there were those who used the condemnation of images for political or economic gain, there certainly must have been those who opposed the icons for fear of idolatry. For those who endorsed the use of icons, idolatry was never an issue. The image was not an object of worship. It was a vehicle to enhance the faith of the viewer by reminding him or her of holy people or events. In subtle ways, the iconoclast controversy may not yet be settled.

PART II
THE MIDDLE AGES

8 Medieval Highs and Lows

Middle age has always been a popular topic for consideration. Books have been written on the types of crises that can be expected. It's an in-between time, between younger and older life. Many people seem to hesitate about which of the two directions to choose. A choice is not really necessary; middle age has glories and problems of its own.

The same is true of the era in history known as the Middle Ages, the days of knights and chivalry, of craftsmen and guilds, of crusaders and castles. We still walk in the shadow of thirteenth-century Gothic architecture, take for granted the idea of a university, and are mystified by the art of masters.

As time progresses and new social customs emerge, the experiences of the past always take on intrigue. In the eighteenth century — a time of classical thought — the precise and lofty idealism of ancient Greece was regarded as an excellent example of a truly developed culture. Later, in the nineteenth century, when people reacted against the precision of mathematical detail and a more romantic spirit took hold, the paragon of ideal culture shifted from ancient history to the Middle Ages. The dreamt-about days, when honor reigned supreme and unicorns were woven into the tapestry of life, seemed closer to true human nature than logical but inanimate detail.

The thirteenth century — a celebrated segment of the Middle Ages — has been called the greatest of all centuries. A partial list of the accomplishments of that time indicates why some scholars hold that opinion. From that century we have inherited so many gifts:

- *The beginnings of the great universities* — Salerno, Bologna, Paris, Oxford, Cambridge, and other French, Italian, and Spanish universities;
- *The organization of the great craft guilds* — a system of technical instruction and a fraternity of artisans in the same trade;
- *The growth of great art* — the legacy of Gothic architecture, an appreciation of the human form in painting, the poetic and rhythmic expression of the great Latin hymns and the invention of part music, the rise of Dante's great drama and the morality play, national epics including *El Cid, Nibelungenlied,* and *The Legend of King Arthur and His Knights;*
- *The refinement and growth of a legal system* — the Magna Carta and common law, the codification of Canon Law, and university commentaries on the law of the land;
- *The flowering of great saints* — Saint Louis, King of France and Crusader; Saint Thomas Aquinas, the theologian; Saint Dominic, Saint Francis, and Saint Clare, all founders of great religious orders; Saint Elizabeth of Hungary, the woman of charity;
- *The expansion of territorial horizons* — the development of the science of geography, Marco Polo's travels, development of commerce among the peoples.

By the thirteenth century, the Dark Ages had come to an end. Western culture would not only survive but would emerge as a great humanizing force for the generations to follow. Europe was coming out of a depression, and the culture gloried in the newfound prosperity. It seemed that the happy days were back again!

Not all were comfortable with the new discoveries. Growth is never without some pain. Nor would the time be free from some incorrect judgment by those in authority; but judgment is always limited by vision, and a large perspective can only come with time.

Study of the events of the Middle Ages is a study of the history of the Church, for it was involved in every aspect of the European world in those days. The Church had carried Western culture through the days of the barbarian invasion, had converted the invading hordes, and had cultured them into people of the Renaissance. Now society and Church were bursting forth into new growth together.

9 Saint Francis of Assisi

In almost two thousand years of living the teachings of the Lord Jesus, few lives of the saints are so capable of capsulizing the spirit of the Savior as the life of the great Saint Francis of Assisi. His personality taps the deepest source of human existence, and his robes still represent the best qualities in human nature — the values of brotherhood, respect for the earth, and the gentle love of God. There's nothing artificial about Saint Francis, no layers that have to be penetrated before one can see the heart.

Francis is probably best known for his "love affair" with Lady Poverty. He loved to have nothing. Francis' freedom of spirit and conviction about the blessings of possessing nothing were demonstrated one day in Assisi. He had decided to give the control of his life to the providence of the Lord. Francis stood before the bishop of his hometown. He professed his intention; and to show his determination, Francis laid all his worldly wealth at the feet of the bishop, including the clothing he wore on his back. He wished to have nothing; and, released from the burdens that possessions bring, Francis danced naked down the street, unattached and free.

Although Francis always showed concern for the poor, often angering his merchant father, he did not break from his expected role of working in the family business until he was 26 years old. In the year 1206, while reading the gospel, he heard the call to rebuild the Church of God. This he did by laying stone in a decayed chapel. In time, he would realize that the call was to do more than repair a building. The Lord blessed Francis with very important work, to build his *real* Church, the People of God who lived in the city. Francis never became a priest. A powerful preacher, he spoke the language of the people and was poetic besides. It was from his experience of God and the example of his lifestyle that he led many to holiness. He had heard the call to rebuild God's Church.

Francis was a magnet of a man, and others were drawn to follow him. From this group of followers would grow a new family of friars and nuns and lay people known as the Franciscans.

Francis was different from the preachers the people had known before him. He came from the new class of merchants and craftsmen that formed the city. The monasteries of the already established orders were usually located in the country, where the monks could live a life of dedication without distraction. But many of them had begun to lose contact with the people, especially the new class of people that was developing in the cities. The craftsmen and merchants of the city wanted to hear the gospel in their own terms. They were neither noble, knight, nor peasant; and Francis understood their special needs. Francis' love for poverty deeply touched men and women who spent so much energy trying to become comfortable through the things their newfound money could buy. His life was a constant reminder of higher values.

Francis owned nothing, but in his poverty he possessed everything. He called the sun, brother; the moon, sister; and the earth, mother. Wild animals became his friends.

In the absence of material preoccupations, there was room in Francis' heart for God to enter. And the Lord poured forth his Spirit. Francis so identified himself with Jesus that he suffered the wounds of the Lord's Passion, the stigmata, in his hands and feet and side. Wounds so painful brought Francis greater joy as he became one with his Savior.

Francis was one of the gems of the early Middle Ages, and his response to God corresponded to his time; but he is still an inspiration and consolation to the twentieth century. Some things never grow old.

10 The Crusades

Over the course of centuries, the meaning of a word can change. Such a word is *crusader*. In modern usage, the word could refer to a member of a high school basketball team or an enthusiast who wants to change society for the better. In the Middle Ages, however, the word referred to those soldiers who "took the Cross" and went to the Holy Land to wage war with the Moslems. The war cry and the goal of the crusader was to open the city of Jerusalem to the pilgrim. A "war of religion" may be foreign to our way of thinking, but for almost two hundred years (1096-1291) thoughts of being a part of so holy a cause occupied the minds of peasants and kings.

A visit to the place where our Savior lived and died was the dream of the faithful in the Middle Ages. To pray in the cave of Bethlehem, to stand in the room of the Last Supper, to walk the Way of the Cross was akin to getting into the skin of the Messiah. These journeys were no first-class tours but voyages of danger and hardship, undertaken because of the rich blessings they promised. Dreams, graces, and penances were taken away when the ruling Moslems closed Palestine to pilgrims.

But the crusader had more than merely a religious motivation. Politics entered the picture. Bored populations were sparked with hopes of excitement and honor; and feudal lords entertained thoughts of increased wealth and new lands. For the papacy, the Crusades offered a chance to assume a more important role in the course of world events. The threat to the East and the great Byzantine civilization made the emperor in Constantinople turn to the West (Rome) for help. The pope saw the possibility of reunion. Not only might the new war bring wealth to the warrior but, in the process, the heretic could be conquered and the schismatic be reunited. How could anyone resist such a cause!

And so the Crusades were under way. From the first they were doomed to difficulty. The cause was preached with such fervor that fantasies of glory filled the mind. An army of common folk, with no training for battle, began the march toward the Holy City. The People's Crusade, as it was called, sustained by a dream, was the first to arrive at Asia Minor and the first to be defeated.

The "real" crusader army, made up of knights and foot soldiers, did not arrive until several months later. Members of this mighty group made up the actual First Crusade, and they eventually reached the city of Jerusalem. In the next two hundred years, seven Crusades set out for the Holy Land. Their story unfolds like waves on the sea, the ups and downs of lands conquered and lost and conquered and lost again. In the end, the crusaders were driven from the land in 1291.

Although the military progress of the Crusades was noteworthy, their Christianity was questionable. The strife that arose among the leaders and their followers, the plunder and slaughter the victors visited upon the conquered territories, and the short-lived duration of the ideals demonstrate the weakness of the human condition.

Were the Crusades successful? For a short period of time, pilgrimages were restored; much of the advanced culture of the East was brought to Europe; and a few heroes were made. But, in general, they were unsuccessful. The Moslem was not impressed with the barbarian spirit of the Christian invader nor were the Orthodox reunited with Rome. The separations, in fact, only grew wider. For us, the name crusader may carry with it a romantic, almost self-righteous, noble connotation. In part the nuance may be fitting; but it is likewise necessary to balance this thought with one of the great lessons of the Crusades — that even the best can be compromised when ideals are sacrificed to temporary gain.

11 The Black Death

In October 1347, . . . Genoese trading ships put into harbor . . . with dead and dying men at the oars. . . . The diseased sailors showed strange black swellings. . . . The swellings oozed blood and pus and were followed by spreading boils and black blotches on the skin from internal bleeding. The sick suffered severe pain and died quickly within five days of the first symptoms. . . . Depression and despair accompanied the physical symptoms, and before the end "death is seen seated on the face."

This horrible description of the bubonic plague from the novel *Distant Mirror* and the sheer nber of people who died from the disease make it easy to understand why the Black Death was thought to herald the end of the world. Almost 24,000,000 people died from it. If a disease were to kill the same proportion of the world's population today, 1,587,300,000 people would die. We can only imagine the horror that must have taken hold of the population. "One man shunned another. . . . Kinsfolk held aloof, brother was forsaken by brother, oftentimes husband by wife; nay, what is more, and scarcely to be believed, fathers and mothers were found to abandon their own children to their fate, untended, unvisited as if they had been strangers" (Boccaccio's description of events in Florence).

Ignorance of medical science further complicated the horror of the bubonic plague. The real carriers of the disease — rats and fleas — were not suspected. Instead, people tended to blame it on the "wrath of God." The evil of the human race must have been too much even for God to tolerate! The plague was thought to be a punishment for sin! As a result, an already exaggerated sense of guilt was confirmed by the external suffering.

The Church is made up of human beings and thus responds to situations with limited perception. Most fourteenth-century theologians, trying to spiritualize the horrors of the Black Death, could only conclude that all earthly ambition was vanity; only the afterlife had meaning. But other conclusions were also put forward! Perhaps this disaster had explanations other than the "wrath of God." Perhaps it did not, in fact, have anything to do with punishment from God. Some scholars see in this kind of thinking the advent of modern scientific thought.

The plague had other effects upon the Church. After the disease had passed, the Church was found to be wealthier. With the threat of death surrounding every household, many of the wealthier citizens offered substantial donations to the Church as a "sin offering" in the hope of forestalling the horrible fate from their household. Also evident was a growing spirit of anticlericalism. The priests suffered personal attacks. Too many of them had abandoned their posts in the moment of crisis; some had failed to minister to the dying, a sin that was not easily forgiven.

In the end, the Black Death was too monumental to allow definite conclusions; the sufferings could not be explained by the mind. Only symbol could capture the terror. Death took on a shape of its own; it was personified as a skeleton with hourglass and scythe. It had respect for no person; pauper or king, all were subject.

The Church, like every other institution of that day, suffered greatly from the Black Death. Not only could it not fully comprehend what had taken place but there were many failures in action. As a result, the Church would need time to recover and continue the journey through history.

12 The Inquisition

"Heresy!" The word still has a bad sound to it. It not only means that the truth is not contained in the message but that it is dangerous to one's spiritual health. When the structure of society itself depends upon everyone accepting the message, heresy is still more dangerous. It spells rebellion and threatens the stability of culture. For the welfare of the State, then, heresy would have to be combated directly; and in the Middle Ages it was attacked by a court known as the Inquisition.

The Inquisition was given a formal constitution by Pope Gregory IX in 1231, and from that time onward its courts became more and more powerful. In fact, they became aggressive; eventually the judge could bring suit against anyone rumored to be heretical. The accused could not challenge the testimony of "witnesses," for they remained anonymous; and lawyers would not help the accused for fear of being considered accomplices. Penalties for conviction of the accused varied. For minor offenses, penances and pilgrimages were ordered; more severe punishments ranged from imprisonment for converted heretics, to death, carried out by the State, for obstinate and unrepentant heretics.

The Inquisition, as a general phenomenon, reached its height in the middle of the thirteenth century; however, the infamous Spanish Inquisition continued for several centuries. The same authority of Rome, which originally granted the permit for the court to begin, was responsible for its demise.

The Inquisition is a dark chapter in Church history. Even today, one who wishes to condemn the Catholic Church hurls the red-flag word *Inquisition* as an accusation of the institution gone amiss, interfering with the love of God.

Perhaps the Inquisition does connote just that! History is made up of many happenings that, superficially at least, seem preposterous to us. To better understand the Inquisition, we have to place it in the world view of its own day, not to justify misguided actions but to locate events in proper perspective.

Society always rests on a delicate balance. In our modern culture, for instance, the balance of world power is put forth as an explanation for the buildup of arms, the doctrine of deterrence. One nation must not become so strong that all will have to bow to it. Future generations may admire or condemn this conviction. Time alone will judge the logic of this theory with the distance needed for sure conclusions, but we will only be judged rightly if future generations understand the reasons behind the actions.

In the thirteenth century, the Inquisition seemed justified. Society was being weakened at its very foundation. The intimate union that existed between Church and State made it impossible to attack one without inflicting an equal wound on the other. In the Inquisition, both Church and State responded to a perceived threat. The purpose of this court was to detect heresy and, if possible, bring the heretic back to the fold of orthodox doctrine. If conversion was not effected by the trial, the State was to inflict punishment on those who persisted in their error. It was better to make the sinner suffer the torture to win contrition than to allow the soul to suffer eternal punishment in the fires of hell.

When the greatest good an individual possessed — salvation — was in danger, the greatest powers available were logically used both for the good of the individual and the good of the society itself. The threat of heresy was met and the Inquisition became a fact of history.

PART III
THE REFORMATION

13 Luther and Other Reformers

A bit more than five hundred years ago, on November 10, 1483, in the town of Eisleben, Germany, Martin Luther was born. Both for those who revere him as Reformer and for those who condemn him, Luther is significant. And if, as one historian has stated, "we must overcome history by history," it is necessary for us to know about these years to mend the divided state of Christianity that we experience today.

Luther was a man — a complex combination of insight and stubbornness, of fervor and scrupulosity, of sensitivity and determination. He lived in a specific moment of history, and had to interpret his world from that perspective. So, too, did the Church of Rome. And the two did not meet. It is said that Luther had not intended to begin a new denomination; but neither could he tolerate some of the situations he experienced. Too late did the Catholic Reform look at its theological definitions and discipline. The time of dialogue passed.

A few basic facts about Luther's biography might help to place him in perspective. Luther lived an ordinary enough life in his early days. He was talented and dedicated. His education was directed toward becoming a lawyer, but he changed his major and entered the Augustinian monastery at Erfurt. There he lived an exemplary life as a monk, was ordained a priest, and received a doctorate in Sacred Scripture. His academic career flourished at the university in Wittenberg, where he was highly instrumental in establishing a first-class educational institution.

Luther was an academician, but above that he was a pastor. His heart was with the people, and his concern was that the Good News of Jesus Christ be preached. Where this was done, he taught, the Church could be found. "Church" was not, for him, primarily founded on obedience to Rome.

In a highly institutionalized system, these words were suspect. They threatened the papacy itself. Added to this threat were further rumblings. Luther condemned, in his own direct and sometimes insulting style, the selling of indulgences (a means of substantial income) and mandatory celibacy for the clergy. He urged the use of the vernacular in religion and reception of the Eucharist under both species. Eventually, he restated how Christ was present in the Eucharist; he taught that only Baptism and the Eucharist qualified as sacraments. What began for Luther as a Church reform developed into a change in doctrine.

In some countries, the impact of the other Reformers was of a greater magnitude than those called forth by Luther. These men envisioned a change not only of Church doctrine and practice but also of society itself. It was primarily these men who gave Protestantism the strong ethical rigidity that would bring Puritanism to New England centuries later.

John Calvin (born July 10, 1509) is an important character in the Reformation. His genius was evidenced in his ability to organize the doctrines of the Reformed Church into the famous *Institutes of the Christian Religion*. Some historians have compared the importance of this book for Protestantism to the honored place held by Saint Thomas Aquinas' *Summa Theologica* in Catholic theology. By the end of the century, this Reformed Church was the best organized and strongest opponent of the Catholic Church in Europe. The new body of believers was international in character and led by a group of highly dedicated clergy who knew what they wished to accomplish.

The Church of Rome reacted to the Reformation in a variety of ways, but usually from an authoritarian perspective. The influences of the Reformation would eventually force a Catholic Counter-Reformation, the Council of Trent (1545-1563); but by that time the corrections and clarifications would be too late and too little to suit the Reformers. The division had become a reality, a fact that still touches us today.

14 Nationalism and the Church

In our human desire to organize information, we like to put things in categories. Of course, we realize that such generalizations are often inaccurate, but we do it nonetheless. Even with the global mobility and mass communication we have today, many people still tend to affiliate certain nationalities with certain church denominations. People with Polish, Italian, or Spanish surnames are usually presumed to be Catholic, while there is less certainty of religion about those with Arabic, African, or Oriental family names. There is some foundation for these assumptions; few territories in times past had room for more than one religion. Belonging to a particular church was part of one's nationality. (In some places, this is still true today.)

This interplay of nationality and religion was important in the sixteenth century. From the 1100s to the 1600s powerful monarchs controlled their particular domains, providing law and defending their people against any enemies. In return they collected taxes. A feeling of common history emerged as part of the group identity. The people eventually felt they had a stake in the nation and considered themselves as citizens rather than merely subjects. Often, a common enemy served to draw a nation together, and a national language gave the people a way to express their thoughts and world views. Nationalism became their way of living with those around them.

During the years of the Reformation, nationalism played a part in determining the religion of the people. Although most of the people who followed the reforms of Luther were quite sincere, there were some territorial princes who quickly realized that Luther's split with Rome was to their advantage. It decreased the highly organized power of the Church and centralized the authority in the State.

The teachings of the Reformers did not influence all the nations of sixteenth-century Europe, in large part because of nationalism. Spain, for instance, had a long history of withstanding and punishing divergent views through the infamous Inquisition. France's strong central government militated against the splitting of even the practice of religion. Italy was in part under the control of Spain in those years, and the physical closeness of the Papal States helped hold the allegiance of the people. Conflict, including the Peasants' Revolt, which occurred in places where Protestantism had taken root made many of the Catholic rulers suspicious of the Reformation. They were slow to entertain the new ideas in their realm for fear of disorder.

The Reform of Henry VIII in England also makes evident the influence of nationalism in religion. Although some have simplified the split of the Church of England from the Church of Rome by attributing the division to the stubbornness of Henry VIII, who wanted a divorce from his first wife, Catherine of Aragon, the movements of history are seldom so simple. Other forces were at work at the time.

England wanted to control England. Anything foreign was suspect, and the political power of the pope was one of these threats. This division, more than anything else, was an act of State. The king took to himself powers that had always been the right of the papacy. The move was the climax of a tension that had been building for many years: a trend toward an independent national Church. Theologically, the tension was expressed in a debate known as *Conciliarism* — an argument over whether the pope or a general council of the Church held supreme authority.

As the events of the Reformation became part of history, maps could be drawn that subdivided Europe not only by nation but by religion. Nationality and denomination were closely linked.

15 Role of Scripture and Tradition

Protestant and Catholic theology divided at the time of the Reformation in some important matters of dogma. All the Reformers challenged the teaching of the Church of Rome, but each — Luther, Calvin, Zwingli, and others — gave his own nuance to justification, predestination, and sacramental theology. There was, however, one point of disagreement with Rome that almost all the Reformers accepted: The only source of faith is the Bible, and the words of Scripture are to be interpreted by the individual only.

The disagreement on the matter of "Scripture alone" and "private interpretation" is still not completely settled. It is this difference that is at the root of the claim by some fundamentalist denominations that the Catholic Church is unbiblical. Actually, the Sacred Scriptures are at the heart of all Catholic theology and the Church claims the Bible as its own, but we also hold in reverence our tradition — a belief that the Holy Spirit did not stop inspiring God's people when the last author of the Bible put down his quill. A closer look at this issue is certainly worthwhile.

At the time of the Reformation, the authorities in Rome were not receptive to challenge, especially when the objections threatened their security. As a result, when rumblings began, rather than consider the criticism a challenge to growth, the new ideas were censured as rebellion and repudiated harshly. The Reformers, in turn, attacked the teaching authority of the hierarchy and rejected its right to pass judgment.

The reaction of the two groups to each other caused the theological division to become more deeply rooted. The Reformers theologized on the human condition. After the Fall of our first parents in the

Garden of Eden human nature, they claimed, had become totally depraved. It was impossible, they proposed, for human beings — since they were descended from Adam and Eve — to merit any grace. Only the free gift of God, who chose and predestined whomsoever he wished, brought salvation. Even Baptism did not change this depraved condition, and it was, therefore, impossible to trust the discernments of the sinful human mind. Only the divinely inspired Scriptures could serve as a guide for faith. No magisterial pronouncements by Rome could be justified. The only valid approach to the Bible had to be through private interpretation.

In the Catholic theology of the day, the Church as the community of salvation was essential. The community of the redeemed was gathered into the Church by God's saving Word, and the Church, therefore, was the instrument of salvation by which God gathers all to himself. Jesus' sacred teaching, given to the apostles, was preserved, interpreted, and transmitted in the Church to all generations. In a very real sense, therefore, the Bible was the Church's Book. The guarantor of the faithfulness of the Church to Jesus was the gift of the Holy Spirit. For Catholics, then, not only was the Bible a source of revelation but the sacred tradition, given under the inspiration of the Holy Spirit in the Church's history, also revealed God to his people.

Since the Second Vatican Council, a great deal of dialogue has taken place between the Catholic Church and representatives of other churches. With the distance that time provides, some of the differences in the churches have been narrowed or eliminated. This was the wish of the Second Vatican Council and, by the grace of God, it has been marvelously effective. (An update on the progress of these dialogues among the churches is available in the form of five booklets which can be ordered from your local bookstore or from Liguori Publications, Box 060, Liguori, Missouri 63057. They are called the *Reaching Out Series* and consider the dialogue with Lutherans, Episcopalians, Methodists, Presbyterians and Reformed, and Baptists. Each booklet is $1.50. Please include 50¢ for postage and handling for the first item ordered and 25¢ for each additional item.)

16 Catholic Reform

As the sixteenth century progressed, it became more and more obvious that the questions of the Reformers were not going to disappear on their own. A monumental response from the Catholic Church was necessary. The response was the Council of Trent.

Meetings to discuss differences between Catholics and Protestants were held before Trent, but all failed to produce the desired result. In 1522, for instance, Pope Adrian VI attempted a reform. He publicly acknowledged abuses in leadership, but he died before any change could be effected. State leaders also sought reconciliation. Francis I in 1533 and Duke George in 1539 sought to incorporate the spirit of Erasmus in a reunion of divided Christendom.

Erasmus was among the most influential men of past centuries. He has been praised and condemned by both Catholics and Protestants. Pope Paul II offered him a cardinal's hat; yet his words were put on the Index of forbidden books by the Council of Trent. The Reformers praised him as the one who prepared the way for the Reformation by his insightful writings. Calvin and Luther were affected by his constant call to return to the spirit of the gospels and the early Fathers of the Church. All could agree with his condemnation of the ignorance in too many of the clergy and with his warning that the invisible life of the Church might be absorbed by too strong an emphasis on externals. Yet, Protestants also condemned him for not using his prestigious position as a most respected scholar to back up the teachings of the Reform.

Erasmus considered himself dedicated to the gospel; he was always willing to submit to proper authority. His commentary on the eighty-third Psalm (our Psalm 84) stated his basic conviction: The Church is the house of the Lord, and he will restore and mend the Church if it but purge itself of its sins.

Several specific attempts at dialogue were made between the Catholic and Protestant parties. In 1523, at the Diet of Nuremberg, the Protestants demanded a free, Christian Council on German soil. Since free meant without the pope, the authorities in Rome could not agree to such a meeting, and wars between the Emperor of the Holy Roman Empire and the King of France interfered with a meeting on German soil. In 1530, the emperor tried again to reach agreement at the Diet of Augsburg, but to no avail. Every effort to convoke a Council failed. In 1541, a high-water mark of dialogue was attained in the Diet of Regensburg. Like the New Testament episode in which the disciples feared death during a storm at sea, all were urged to turn to Christ for deliverance from the conflict. But as with earlier efforts, nothing came of them.

In 1545, a little more than twenty years after the Diet of Nuremberg, the Council of Trent was finally convoked by Pope Paul III. It continued, with interruptions, for eighteen years.

Trent guided the Catholic Church for the next four hundred years. It met in response to the challenges of the Protestant Reformers and, as a result, the general tone of the Council was defensive. Its purpose was to shoulder up what was tottering due to the attack of enemies.

Trent cast the philosophy and theology of the Church for centuries to come. It restated the centrality of the seven sacraments in Catholic religious practice. It defended whatever the Protestants attacked and condemned those who followed the new teachings. It reconfirmed Latin as the language of the Church and legislated strict liturgical law. It placed restrictions on Catholic dialogue with Protestants and penalized marriages of mixed religion. It established seminaries as a means of instructing the future clergy in true doctrine. Armed with the well-defined direction of the Council of Trent, the Catholic Church had set its direction for the next four centuries.

17 Expanded Missionary Activity

The Foreign Missions may conjure up thoughts of jungles and snakes and primitive, uncivilized peoples. The concept bears some relationship to the truth, depending on the place evangelized and on one's definition of *civilized*. In the sixteenth century, the mission fields, including those of North America, were dangerous and, to the European mentality, in a state of primitive culture.

After the Church suffered the torments of the Reformation, the logical outcome might have been one of retreating to an introspection that would be the opposite of missionary zeal. Such was not the case. The sixteenth and seventeenth centuries evidence an expansion of missionary activity unparalleled to that time, except possibly by Saint Paul's journeys in the very first century of the Church.

The discovery of the new territories of the East and Far East and of North and South America in the previous century caused a new excitement over the possibilities of colonization and conversion.

In the Americas, the missionaries followed the Spanish and Portuguese conquistadors who were able to claim large territories for their nations. These conquerors were not concerned with existing cultures; and although it was often the clergy who held in check the hand of the conqueror, the missionaries were products of their ancestral culture. Conversion dictated the destruction of false religions and the culture that surrounded them. The armies of Europe were effective. By 1511, the Diocese of Santo Domingo (in the West Indies) was established.

Catholicism also came with the French to parts of North America as a majority religion, while in other parts Protestantism would hold sway — at least until the nineteenth century when immigration of a large Catholic population would change the balance.

In the East, missionaries like the famous Saint Francis Xavier sought to convert the peoples of established and developed civilizations. Some of the missionaries proposed adapting Christianity to the cultures of China and India; other missionaries opposed this idea. The debate continued for almost a century until, in 1742, Rome disapproved the adaptation. In the end, Christianity was not firmly established in the East.

Missionary activity had a close relationship to colonization, but the missionaries were not primarily motivated by the goals of national expansion. Their zeal rested on the command of the Savior before his Ascension: ''Full authority has been given to me both in heaven and on earth; go, therefore, and make disciples of all the nations'' (Matthew 28:18-19).

For almost two centuries, missionary activity continued at a feverish pitch. By 1789, the Church had touched almost every corner of the globe through evangelization and emigration. But by that same date, missionary activity was in a state of decline. Most missionaries came from religious orders; and when the religious orders, congregations, and societies suffered suppression, persecution, and decline, as happened in the eighteenth century, the missions suffered. When that occurred, a weakness in the system of earlier centuries became obvious. A sufficient number of native clergy had not been established. As a result, the faithful were left without the sacraments for long periods of time.

One hundred years later, the Church would have a second chance to establish Christianity with a native clergy. Under the pontificate of Gregory XVI, a renewed and more tolerant surge of missionary activity resurfaced and continues to this day. Missiology, the study of the nature, purpose, and methods of evangelization, is now a prominent part of the Church's educational activity. Missionaries, motivated by the command of Ascension Day, zealously seek to bring the message of the gospel to all people in all lands.

PART IV
THE MODERN ERA

18 The Error of Rigorism

Statements of disagreement over theology no longer surprise the average Catholic, but our conflicts, in themselves, need not cause us discouragement. They are only dangerous if they are not handled constructively. Many of the disagreements in past ages have actually spurred great growth in the life of the Church. To get a better perspective on this give-and-take process, think about the seventeenth century.

The debates of that day considered theological issues, but the arguments were not of the kind that only abstract thinkers enjoyed. The questions touched real life: "How can I know if Jesus died for me; and if I am one he died for, how should I live?"

One response to this kind of questioning that has continued to affect Catholic life was Jansenism. It was very close to a Protestant view on the depraved nature of humankind, but it grew within the Catholic Church. This philosophy of Christian life was expressed in 1640 when a book written by a Dutch theologian named Jansen was published under the title of *Augustinus*. He proposed that when God first created human beings he made them good; but after the Fall, human nature became a slave of sin and could no longer do good on its own. Grace was given, however, to the elect few for whom Jesus died. The sign by which a person knew he or she belonged to the elect was a spirit of fear that kept the soul from approaching the sacraments or feeling at peace with God. A spirit of rigorism characterized the practice of the faith.

Jansenism was especially strong in France, but it was not limited to that nation. The teachings took root in other lands, especially when some members of the clergy were expelled from the region and emigrated with the infection to other lands, including North America.

Even after this teaching was condemned by the Church, the gloomy spirit of Jansenism continued to be influential. In fact, there are still remnants of it in the twentieth century!

One who argued against the loveless approach of Jansen and against the notion that Jesus died only for a few, was the great Doctor of the Church, Saint Alphonsus Liguori. He could not let this error go unchallenged. He was too much in love with the God of love.

Alphonsus' attack was two-pronged. For the person in the pew, he wrote books of devotion to revive the hearts that had been frozen in pessimism. Modern readers may find him emotional, but his aim was just that — to put the feeling of love in religion, to remove the idea that remorse was the true Christian spirit. His booklets *Visits to the Blessed Sacrament* and *The Glories of Mary* are two examples of this approach. With marvelous sentiments, he reinstated the burning love of God into the piety of the day. Alphonsus argued that only the love of God, not human rigorism, was capable of curing every vice and developing true virtue.

For the intellectual, Saint Alphonsus wrote his magnificent works of moral theology, in part to combat the errors of Jansenism. So much was his work appreciated that he was named the patron saint of confessors and moral theologians. The school of moral theology in Rome, the Alphonsian Academy, still carries his name.

The Reformation and Counter-Reformation would not end debate in the Christian world. New questions demanded new teachings to answer doubts, and this pattern will probably continue until the end of time. But this is neither a cause for alarm nor for despair. When great problems plague the Church, great saints are raised up to answer the challenge. In searching for answers to pressing questions, under the inspiration of the Holy Spirit, we find God's direction in our lives and in our Church.

19 Period of Rationalism and Romanticism

In the seventeenth and eighteenth centuries, different ways of thinking began to emerge that have influenced our philosophies of life. One glorified the mind, while the other placed emphasis on intuition. These ways of interpreting reality have been called Rationalism and Romanticism.

Rationalism, as its name implies, emphasizes thought; and the era of history when it most strongly emerged is called the Age of the Enlightenment. The Enlightenment was, in part, a reaction against a time of religious wars and persecution. Religion was in such a state of chaos that some dramatic response was inevitable, and it can be seen in the rejection of many of the external aspects of traditional religion.

Rationalism opposed all that appeared to be superstitious in thought or worship. As a result, these centuries tended to be antidogmatic. The Enlightenment demanded the right to question everything. Things that could not be logically proven were not accepted by "enlightened people." This meant, for instance, that life after death, the virgin birth, and the two natures of Christ were not accepted, for they could not be proven scientifically.

The rational approach to life has to its credit many of the great developments of science. At its extreme, however, it led to a neurotic desire for order and control that suppressed freedom for "the people's own good." Before long, a reaction to Rationalism grew in strength.

Romanticism, as the reaction was called, attracted many followers. Wordsworth became its spokesperson. Where Newton, the spokesperson for Rationalism, viewed the world as a well-ordered machine, Wordsworth saw the world as mysterious and full of wonder. Not only do human beings know reality by means of the mind they also know by means of intuition and feeling. The mind views structures; intuition attempts to grasp the nature of things. The mind looks for orderliness; intuition looks for spontaneity in life.

Romanticism taught that spontaneity was the spice of life. Great learning came from "wasting time" daydreaming; and intuition of the heart was thought to be closer to wisdom than anything logic could figure out. As a matter of fact, the basic unity of all creation could only be grasped by intuition.

Romanticism emphasized eternal and spiritual values. It was given to contemplation. Many of the movements of ecology find their roots in this way of thinking. At its pathological extreme, however, romantic thinking could be irresponsible, neglecting both social and political obligation. It believed that being was more important than doing.

During these centuries, the honored positions held by the established institutions of government and Church were eroded and replaced by values that glorified the individual. The inalienable rights granted by nature to every person were incorporated into law. Rationalism's emphasis on the perfectibility of human nature and Romanticism's basic conviction that institutional power needed to be constantly checked underlie the great American and French Revolutions that took place during these centuries.

Both rational and romantic thinking have their place in the Church. Both make valid and necessary contributions to theology. The twentieth century inherited many of the basic beliefs of these movements. Theology moved away from an emphasis solely on the supernatural toward a stress on the importance of religion for the growth of the individual personality. Human thinking and human feeling both emerged as important elements in religious living. These values still influence our lives today.

20 The French Revolution

The French Revolution had more influence on the Catholic Church than any other revolution. One historian stated that the life of the twentieth-century Catholic Church before the Second Vatican Council had been one of reaction to two major historical events — the Reformation in the sixteenth century and the French Revolution at the end of the eighteenth century.

Conditions in France in the late 1700s were strained. Even King Louis XVI, isolated in the privacy of his palace, experienced the tensions. Yielding to popular clamor, he convoked the Estates General, the governing body that represented all groups of people — the nobles, the clergy, and the citizens. For 175 years, the monarchy had been able to rule without the parliamentary body, but at that fateful moment of history, the king had made many compromises to keep the realm afloat. He had lost his supreme power. The effort on the part of the king, however, was not successful. Within two months, the Revolution had begun. On July 14, 1789, a mob stormed the Bastille, and the monarchy eventually fell.

Ending an old regime by revolution was an easier job than establishing a new government. This latter task fell to the National Constituent Assembly, which issued ''The Declaration of the Rights of Man and of the Citizens,'' a constitution guaranteeing individual rights and liberties. A part of the new Constitution affected the Church. Since the Church seemed so closely connected with the king, it fell with the monarchy. In November 1789, Church property was nationalized and dispersed; in February 1790, religious communities were suppressed; in July 1790, the ''Civil Constitution of the Clergy'' was enacted, which separated the clergy from Rome and made them ''ministers'' of the State. (It was during this time that many French priests emigrated to North America rather than split with Rome.)

These were the days of "The Reign of Terror." A concerted effort at dechristianization had begun. No public worship was permitted; clerical garb was forbidden; and churches were desecrated. An attempt was made to replace the Christian religion with the cult of the State. Ceremonies were begun to honor the goddesses Reason and Liberty. Even a calendar was developed on the basis of a ten-day week to make the day of rest and worship a thing of the past.

It was not until the time of Napoleon, forever a practical man who saw the need of religion in his State, that a treaty between Church and State was effected. The treaty took eight months and more than twenty-six drafts to finalize. Napoleon was insistent that although the Church was a reality in France so was the Revolution. The State would serve as the guardian of the religion and not the other way around. The pope was to recognize the Revolution and the fact that the Church life, as it had formerly existed, was changed. Confiscated possessions of the Church would not be returned, but the cults of the State would be ended and the Catholic liturgy would be restored. The Concordat also recognized the right of the pope to appoint bishops, although they had to be from among those nominated by the French government.

The great effect that this Revolution had on the Church derives from the fact that France, sometimes called "The Eldest Daughter of the Church," was so thoroughly Catholic in its culture that the Revolution was devastating. The status quo was rocked at its foundations. A religious state was secularized, and the new philosophy degraded religion and uprooted it from all structures possible. The Church was considered the enemy of progress and citizens' rights. It was a difficult transition: a divine institution adjusting to a new social order.

21 The First Vatican Council

In his treatise *On the Unity of the Church* Saint Cyprian, one of the Fathers of the early Church, urged that those who wanted to believe true dogma should look to Rome for correct doctrine. Through all the generations of Church history the Bishop of Rome has held a place of honor. In the first century Peter, given authority by Jesus himself, settled in Rome. His successors continued to speak with his authority in union with the other successors of the apostles. Finally, at the First Vatican Council in the year 1870, the exact nature of papal infallibility was defined as Church doctrine. Until then papal infallibility had been a concept generally accepted throughout the world, but it had not been clearly defined. Only a few questioned the right of the pope to speak in the name of the infallible Church.

Before the definition of papal infallibility by the First Vatican Council the topic was open for debate. Two opinions were generally held: the ultramontane position, which was interested in bolstering the power of the pope; and the liberal position, which wanted the Church government to become more decentralized.

Early in his career Pius IX might have been more interested in decentralization, but after having bad experiences in ruling the papal states, he drew back into a position that distrusted democratic government. When a council was called to meet in Rome, therefore, most people were cautious about the motives for such a gathering. Was the council merely a political move on the part of the pope?

The position of the pope was suspect, especially to non-Catholics in North America. The pope, as recent as 1864, issued a document called "A Syllabus of Errors" which, among other things, denounced the notion that Church and State should be separate, that there should be absolute freedom of speech and press, and that the State should grant equal toleration of all religions. In the United States, this was the time of the Know-Nothing Party, which was already anti-Catholic to its roots and very distrustful of Rome.

In spite of the suspicion of some, Pope Pius IX convoked the First Vatican Council. For seven months the bishops tackled a most controversial question — the nature of the infallibility of the pope. As the discussion progressed it became clear what Pius IX thought about the topic. Equally apparent was the fact that a vote against papal infallibility would be a vote against the reigning pope. To avoid the conflict some of the bishops withdrew from the Council, using the excuse that war was imminent in France and they should be with their flocks. When the vote on papal infallibility was finally taken, only two bishops present voted against it — the bishop of Cajazzo, Sicily, and the bishop of Little Rock, Arkansas. After the results were tabulated, however, both dissenting voters accepted the outcome of the Council as the direction of the Holy Spirit.

The pronouncement of the First Vatican Council clearly set the boundaries of papal infallibility. The pope was declared infallible only when he made pronouncements *ex cathedra,* to all peoples, on a matter of faith and morals. The definition is so precise that only once in more than one hundred years has papal infallibility been invoked — when the Assumption of Mary was solemnly declared a doctrine of the Catholic Church.

22 Catholics in North America

There is more to the coming of religion to the North American continent than the landing of the Pilgrims at Plymouth Rock. A lot of religious history occurred in North America before the 1600s in places other than the thirteen original American colonies. That history has Catholicism at its center.

Although other nations were definitely involved in the beginnings of European influence in the Americas, three nations were responsible for the majority of the colonization of North America — Spain, France, and England.

The Spanish were the first to make permanent settlements in North America. The empire of that nation extended from South and Central America up into the southern part of the present United States. The French occupied present-day Canada and broad regions of the central and the eastern United States. The English colonized New England. Spain and France were strongly Catholic; the English colonists were, generally speaking, anti-Catholic, though Maryland was established by English Catholics.

In 1521 the Spaniard Juan Ponce de Leon landed in Florida. From that date to the opening of the last California mission in 1823, Spain established colonies and Catholicism in America. Often, there was conflict between the policies of the Church and the State. Though no one would be so naïve as to think there was never error on the side of the Church in these conflicts, it was usually the Church that saw to the preservation of human rights in conflict situations. Churchmen knew the Indians were children of God with immortal souls, and the missionaries made heroic sacrifices to win these people for Christ. In the years of colonization, missions were established throughout the southern United States. There were twenty-one missions in California, as many in Texas, more in Florida, and twice that number in New Mexico. These missions provided protection and instruction to the peoples of the land.

The same conviction influenced the great French missionaries. With equal zeal they brought the faith to people in eastern Canada and to the people of the area around the Great Lakes and the Mississippi Valley in the United States. The heroic stories of the martyrdom of French Jesuits in the 1640s are still some of the most captivating accounts of dedication in the annals of religious history. These ''black robes'' were known in the wilds of both Canada and the United States, and their penetration and mapping of the frontiers provided the information needed for later expeditions. A quick look at names of so many rivers, the great means of travel in those days, and of towns and cities, the places where the populations settled, will reveal the influence of the French and their Catholic faith in the settlement of North America.

The English colonizers were not so united in their faith as were the Spanish and French. Catholics account for only a small minority of the English settlers. Maryland was founded by Catholics for religious freedom in the New World. The Catholics of Maryland were, in general, splendid in their toleration of other denominations, a favor not often returned to the Catholic settlers by other denominations.

This absence of a single denomination in the thirteen original colonies in the United States made a great contribution to the future of the nation. It fostered the principle of religious freedom, a principle with which Catholics are in full accord. The New World offered the possibility of religious freedom in national unities, a sacred trust given to future generations.

23 Immigrant Catholics in the USA

In the nineteenth century the Catholic Church in America took on a new look. Catholics were a small and insignificant denomination in the early 1800s. By the time of the Civil War they had become the largest single denomination in the United States, numbering 3,500,000 people. This swell in numbers was brought about by the large immigration of people, especially from Ireland and Germany. In later generations the influx of Poles, Italians, Slavs, and the Hispanic peoples continued to increase the Catholic population. To many of the more established Americans, Catholic became synonymous with foreign and, as a result of a basic distrust in the unknown, tension increased.

By the time most of the immigrants arrived in the New World they were devoid of funds. Any money the immigrant might have had before the journey to the New World was used in travel expenses. Most had to take menial jobs and live in ghettos with fellow immigrants. The Church served as a single anchor in a topsy-turvy world.

The great increase in numbers was a challenge to the American Catholic Church. One church historian describes the situation in terms of human development: "Like adolescence, with its spurts, the task was to stay alive and to develop correctly." Luckily, division made by ethnic background did not cause disunion in the Church. The handbook of belief for the Catholic was the Tridentine faith of the catechism, and this faith transcended national borders.

One reaction by non-Catholics to this wave of newcomers, which was particularly odious in the land of the free, was that of the Nativists. Some who had lived in the United States for a longer period than the new arrivals thought of themselves as the true Americans. The immigrant was, to them, a threat to democracy and religion. Rumors began to be spread that the pope or some foreign monarch was plotting to usurp power in the United States. Outrageous accusations were made against the nuns and priests as living sanctioned immoral lives. These campaigns of prejudice were influential, particularly with the uneducated.

As experience in prejudice grew, more sophisticated anti-Catholic propaganda also surfaced. Catholics were denounced as "Bible burners." This idea became the focus of the new crusade against the Catholic Church. The organization of prejudice would eventually become so extensive that a political party, with prejudice as its uniting force, was formed. These Know-Nothings, as they were called, exercised various forms of violence against the Catholics but when questioned, "knew nothing about it."

To the Catholics, the doubt of their loyalty was confusing. At the Fourth Provincial Council in 1840 the American bishops clearly stated that the Catholic religion did not interfere with American freedom. "We disclaim all right to interfere with your judgment in political affairs of our common country, and are far from entertaining the wish to control you in the constitutional exercise of your freedom."

More than a century has passed since these events took place, but, strange to say, somewhere not too far below the surface an anti-Catholic bias still exists in the United States. Many are quite ready to believe these same irrational statements about Catholics. Even Catholics themselves are made to question their allegiance to a Church that is put forward as in error. While constructive criticism serves for growth, prejudice has no right to stand. It must never be condoned. An awareness of our past history can serve to create a higher consciousness today.

24 Impact of Vatican II

No event in the recent history of the Church has had such a profound effect upon the lives of the Catholic people as the Second Vatican Council. On January 25, 1959, Pope John XXIII made his surprise announcement that he intended to convoke a general council of the whole Church. No such assembly had taken place since the First Vatican Council in 1869-70, and Pope John intended to "open the window" to allow the Holy Spirit to blow afresh upon his Church.

John XXIII's opened window did take place, and his spirit pervaded the deliberations of the Council members. After four years of preparations the first session of the Council took place on October 11, 1962. In the opening address Pope John set the tone. This Council was to be pastoral; it was more concerned with the shepherding of the People of God in the streets and jungles of the world than with correcting doctrinal error. In this sense, Vatican II was more practical than theoretical. The image of Christ the Good Shepherd was more prominent than Christ the Teacher, though many teachings emerged from the Council.

For more than three years the bishops of the world, in union with the Holy Father, discussed and debated weighty Church matters. Also present were invited guests — laity and clergy who were experts in certain fields or were representatives of non-Catholic denominations and non-Christian faiths. It was a mighty assembly!

A quick listing of the documents that emerged from these discernings serves to show the amount of material covered in the deliberations: The Church, Revelation, The Liturgy, The Church in the Modern World, Communication, Ecumenism, Eastern Churches, The Office of Bishop, Priestly Formation, Religious Life, The Laity,

Priests, The Missions, Education, Non-Christians, and Religious Freedom.

The Second Vatican Council was, indeed, a monumental moment in the history of the Catholic Church. It began a new era in the lives of Catholics and demanded a time of major adjustment for many. The Church's understanding of itself changed, the way of worship was altered, and even the very relationship of Church to world was transformed. All of these required new thinking. Yet, probably for most Catholics in North America, the greatest shift ushered in by the changes was a new role for the laity.

"There are certain things which pertain in a particular way to the laity, both men and women, by reason of their situation and mission" (The Church, #30). This is a work that no cleric could adequately perform. Members of the laity are the leaven of the world, lifting all creation to God by active involvement in social and family concerns. Holiness is not an escape from reality but a deeper dive into life lived in society. "The laity, by their very vocation, seek the kingdom of God by engaging in temporal affairs and by ordering them according to the plan of God" (The Church, #31).

The role of the laity is evident not only in the workplace and the home but in the Church too. Ministries, at one time the exclusive service of the priest, have been properly distributed to the People of God. "As sharers in the role of Christ the Priest, the Prophet, and the King, the laity have an active part to play in the life and activity of the Church. Their activity is so necessary within church communities that without it the apostolate of the pastors is generally unable to achieve its full effectiveness" (The Apostolate of the Laity, #10).

It takes a good number of years before the work of a Council filters into the life of the Church. The effects of Vatican II will eventually touch the lives of all Catholics. God is still at work forming his people.

Conclusion

In these pages we have looked at various moments in history in order to better understand how the modern Church evolved. Long-standing traditions and practices develop neither in a vacuum nor in a theoretical framework. They are worked out of real life situations.

That which has been given to the Church is the divine life of God. The resurrected Lord lives in his Church. "He has put all things under Christ's feet and has made him thus exalted, head of the church, which is his body" (Ephesians 1:23). The Body of Christ, responding to the events, the crises, and the questions of history, has evolved into an institution rich in tradition and wise with experience. "For faith throws a new light on everything, manifests God's design for man's total vocation, and thus directs the mind to solutions that are fully human" (Church in the Modern World, #11). Church history makes evident the divine and the human elements that make up our Catholic heritage.

To grasp the lessons of Church history it is necessary to understand the interplay of faith with human history, for both play vital parts in the traditions, teachings, and practices that have emerged. Having looked at a number of events from past history, is it possible to look to the future with a broader perspective?

While we neither know the future course of events nor fully anticipate the power of the Holy Spirit, which "blows where it wills," we can look ahead with more awareness because we know what has taken place in the past.

From our wealth of history and the accumulation of experience over the past nineteen hundred plus years, we know that God will remain with us, as he promised, "until the end of the world" (Matthew

28:20). No matter what may happen, with the divine life of God in the Church and the powers of the human mind and heart, we will be able to find a solution to all questions and difficulties. This does not guarantee freedom from all error in the ordinary course of events, but it does give a reason for hope. Nations may totter, persecutions may resume, heresy may make new inroads; but by the power of God and the strength of human fortitude and wisdom, the course of history will always eventually be set straight.

Church history also teaches us the solemn obligation we human beings have for responding to the signs of the times. Many wrong turns have been made that have caused great suffering and division. We, too, can promote turmoil by our limited vision. On the other hand, we have at our disposal, under the direction of the Holy Spirit, the ability to bring about a better world by our daily responses. Through our reaction to events the Kingdom of God can be increased or decreased in our world.

Finally, Church history shows us that we make our pilgrim way to heaven by living the nitty-gritty. Our perfection is not accomplished in abstraction but by the trivia that make up our day. We may dream of the big break, the great conversion, the moment to change all moments, but actual history is made up of the trends set by the many small steps taken in response to the circumstances of our lives. Significant happenings are only the accumulation of many insignificant details.

Church history, in the end, is the working out of the details of God's plan for the coming of the Kingdom in our world: ''God has given us the wisdom to understand fully the mystery, the plan he was pleased to decree in Christ, to be carried out in the fullness of time: namely, to bring all things in the heavens and on earth into one under Christ's headship'' (Ephesians 1:9-10).